Salt Lines

A Poetry Collection

T.B. Wittkofsky

CONTENTS

DEDICATION

For the ocean, my first teacher.

Thank you for teaching me humility before depth.

To breathe when I cannot see bottom.

To surrender without quitting.

To read the weather, not the rumor.

To respect the rip and ask for help.

To let go, then return with the tide.

To keep moving in small, honest strokes.

That quiet can hold me when language cannot.

That light, even a faint one, is enough to steer by.

That survival is a practice, not a headline.

That I can be carried for a while and still learn to swim.

That home is the shore you choose again.

For all the ways you almost kept me, and the greater lesson that I could come back.

ACKNOWLEDGEMENTS

Jake,

Thank you for opening the door to poetry for me. You put a notebook in my hands and said, write. You read the first rough lines without flinching. You noted the parts that were honest and told me, keep that. You pushed me to share the work when I wanted to hide it.

You were the first to believe in these poems. You sat through long drafts. You texted back at 2 a.m. You said, send the submission, then reminded me to try again when the rejection came. You gave straight feedback. Clear, kind, specific. You helped me cut what didn't serve the poem and trust what did.

When life went dark, you stayed. You picked up the phone. You checked in. You made sure I ate and slept. You kept the days moving when I could not. You reminded me that a line a day counts. You told me I could get to tomorrow.

So much of what lives in these pages started with your yes. Your steady presence shaped my voice, my habits, and my grit. If someone finds a line here that helps, it traces back to you.

For the notebooks, the rides, the coffee, the late edits, the early mornings, and the years of support, thank you. This book stands because you stood with me.

A NOTE FROM T.B.
BEFORE YOU READ

THIS COLLECTION IS RAW on purpose. I wrote these poems to say what I felt, when I felt it, why I felt it. I kept the edges. I kept the parts that do not land clean. That is the truth of it.

I believe only the poet can edit work like this. Outside edits can smooth the voice until it is no longer mine. Each cut changes meaning. Each change shifts a feeling I need to keep. I alone can decide what to keep and what to let go.

Form follows emotion here. Not rules. Line breaks, punctuation, repetition, and white space are choices. So are silence and abrupt stops. Some poems bend grammar. Some repeat a word until it carries weight. None of that is a mistake. It is intent.

Poetry is expression. Poets sit outside the box on purpose. We try things. We risk being messy in order to be clear. I embrace that. I accept the risk that not every line will please. I want every line to be honest.

Read this with an open mind. Let the rhythm set the pace. If a poem feels rough, that is part of its work. If one piece hits hard, let it. If another feels quiet, let that too. This is me, in the form that best holds what I needed to say.

BROKEN PARTS

I STARE INTO THE mirror,
and wonder who broke first,
me,
or the reflection.
Was this morning real?
Or did I make it up?
Am I still asleep,
dreaming of a life that feels
separated from reality?
They say perception is reality.
But what if perception lies?
What if this world is sculpted
not from solid stone or metal,
but from malleable clay
of fear and need,
molded in midnight

by the trembling hands of a child
inside a grown man's chest?
Maybe the sky isn't blue,
they're just a shade
I decided meant calm
after too many black nights
where the walls pulsed in red.
Maybe smiles
are just masks we assign
to the shapes we need to trust.
Is love real,
or is it just gravity I dressed up
to keep myself from floating away?
Some mornings I wake
and the sun tastes rich like gold,
warm, nourishing,
almost divine.
Other days, it blinds.
And I wonder
if it's the sky that changes
or just my eyes.
I hear voices
that sound a lot like memory
and a little like doubt.
One says:
"Life is a test."
Another replies:
"No, it's a painting,

and your brush is broken."
And a quieter voice,
the one I trust most,
whispers:
"It's both.
And neither.
And more."
There are days I feel held together
by an unseen cosmic thread,
a tapestry held loosely
by gods I don't believe in
but still talk to
when the rest of the world is quiet.
I find answers
not in temples or books,
but in the way
a thunderstorm
feels like a hymn,
or how my dog's sigh
is more honest than any sermon.
I don't claim truth.
I claim experience.
And even that wavers.
Sometimes,
my thoughts wear masks,
some shout louder than logic,
some whisper darker than night.
They shape the room,

shift the floor beneath my feet.
I walk carefully.
Reality,
is often a tightrope
strung between two truths
that disagree with each other
violently.
Is the world falling apart,
or am I?

Does anything matter
if the feeling is always the same?
I ask the stars for answers,
but they've seen too much.
Their silence
is either sacred
or cruel.
Some days,
I believe in purpose.
Others,
I believe I created purpose
just to stay alive.
And still
I wake.
I write.
I love.
I ache in ways
that prove I am here.

SALT LINES

Even if "here"
is something I invented
to make the pain feel noble.
So maybe none of this is real.
Maybe it's all a construct
of electrical sparks and survival.
But if this illusion holds me,
if it lets me feel beauty,
if it lets me whisper
"I am still here"
even when the fog rolls in,
then maybe that's real enough.
Maybe truth
isn't about what is,
but what we need
to keep going.
And I...
I need this.
Even the broken parts.
Especially the broken parts.

GRACE

DROWNING

before I saw the water.
The surface was above
but it felt so far,
like a concept someone else invented
to explain a feeling I couldn't master.
Most wouldn't call it drowning.
Most wouldn't call it anything.
The somber silence doesn't scream.
It simmers.
It becomes a second skin.
And eventually,
you stop remembering
you're not supposed to live
beneath the pressure.
Then came

SALT LINES

Grace.
Not golden, not glowing,
not some mythic fire burning in a storm.
A tug.
A shift.
A question asked without sound:
"What if you didn't have to go through this alone?"
It didn't come in lightning.
It came in the way chaos quieted
when Grace settled around me.
In how I forgot to be afraid
for the span of a laugh.
At the intersection of ache and accident,
I wasn't ready
but I was unraveling.
And maybe that was the point.
Never asked to become whole.
Never measured the missing pieces.
Just sat with Grace
to show off the sacred relics
of battles I'd survived.
Some people see storms
and stay indoors.
When I see mine,
we walk straight in
without an umbrella,
barefoot,
open-palmed.

And it wasn't love.

Not then.

Not the kind they write about in cheap paperbacks

with perfectly timed eye contact.

It was quieter.

More defiant.

It was an inkling of belief

where none had been planted.

I used to think my mind was a maze

with no center.

Just walls and mirrors

and rooms where every voice

sounded like mine

but hated me more than the last.

I was never offered a map.

I was brought a chair

to sit beside myself.

Let me rage.

Let me weep.

Let me forget how to speak

and still be heard.

Grace didn't light the path.

It made it okay

that I was crawling.

There are moments

when my pulse becomes a riddle,

and my thoughts turn

from prayer

to punishment.
Never tried to fix it.
Just handed me my own breath
like it was something worth keeping.
I have splintered
in more ways than languages can hold.
Split myself across timelines,
with each version of me
trying to earn their worth.
When they were found,
the loud one,
the numb one,
the one who laughs too hard at funerals
just to feel something,
Grace labeled them beautiful.
The weight that doesn't crush,
but roots.
The force that tells your bones
you're still here
even when your mind
won't believe it.
Divinity wears many faces.
I found it in Grace,
when I couldn't find myself.
I've built shrines
from coffee spoons and apologies.
Offered worship
in the way I remember songs

and the exact cadence of breathing
when consumed by sleep
after being carried through
yet another storm
that knew my name.
My sacred text
written in glances
and unfinished sentences.
The thread
I hold when the world frays.
And sometimes,
sometimes I pull too hard.
Sometimes I beg it to snap
just to see
if Grace really remains.
But it holds.
God, it holds.
And that thread,
that impossibly quiet,
unshakably steady
thread,
has become the proof
that maybe I was never broken.
Just waiting
for Grace
in the sound of shattered things.

LIGHTKEEPER

THE STORM CAME SLOWLY.

    Not as rumbling thunder,

    but as deafening silence.

    It grew from the cracks between my ribs,

    wrapped fingers 'round my shallow breath,

    and whispered that I wasn't built to last.

    Made me believe my broken was permanent.

    Convinced me my story would be a footnote

    in someone else's lesson

    on how not to become a failure.

    But then there was the light.

    Not lightning.

    An ember.

    A flicker when all the other candles blew out.

    The light that didn't chase the shadows away,

    but sat with me until they made room.

I screamed into the abyss,

and it answered softly:

"You're still here. So fight."

Never asked to be perfect.

The light illuminated the chaos

as I navigated each tidal shift

until I saw myself as something more

than the reflection in my shipwrecked ruin.

Every voice held hands in protest

and the demons unionized.

Crazed shouting over uneasy whispers,

as depression drug rusted chains through my spirit's marrow.

Physically.

Soulfully.

Tired.

The light became my mirror

and I started to see hope

in the ruins of what once was.

The light didn't carry the sun,

it was the sun.

Burning with a warmth

that didn't ask why I ached,

just stayed when the ache arose.

A compass in the chaos.

A psalm sung in every language.

The proof that divinity isn't found in gods,

but in the things which refuse to let go of you

when you're slipping from yourself.

SALT LINES

All the books.
All the truths.
I've seen the divine
in every whisper of wind,
every crackling fire,
every tear that refused to fall.
No scripture felt more sacred
than the way the light touched my cheek
when my eyes wouldn't open
because I was too afraid of waking.
I am not whole.
I am here.
The light keeps burning
while I correct the course.
And if the darkness comes for me again,
with its scythe in one hand
and my name in the other,
know this:
I will not go.
Because I've felt what light feels like
when it warms you enough
to pull you home.

IF ANYONE ASKS

I AM TIRED

    in a way that sleep cannot solve.

    The kind of tired that lives in marrow,

    beneath the armor I still wear

    for people

    who never asked how heavy it is.

    They see the smile.

    They see the cheers.

    They see the safe harbor.

    They don't see

    the tide

    swallowing me whole.

    I pour and pour and pour

    into hands that never notice

    I've been empty for miles.

    They toast their success

with the pieces of me
I no longer have the strength to hold.
I am the foundation,
the lifter,
the soft place to fall.
But my knees are bruised
from catching people
who never turned around
to see if I stood back up.
I clap for their wins
with fingers bloodied
from clawing my way out of holes
they didn't know I fell into.
I whisper light into midnight
for strangers,
but mine stays unlit.
Somewhere, I traded my matchstick
for a candle.
They call me strong.
I call it survival
masquerading as happiness.
There's a storm
that doesn't sound like thunder.
It murmurs inside me,
rewriting truth with every gust.
Telling me I'm too much
and never enough
in the same whisper.

A mosaic
glued together by obligation.
Shiny, maybe.
Whole, never.
Some days
I am the sun
sharing its warmth.
Some days
I am the cold eclipse
no one remembers.
I believe
in fire
in breath
in the sound of rain
on the tin roof at 3 a.m.
I've prayed to them all.
Even the quiet ones.
Especially the quiet ones.
Not for rescue,
but for rest.
Just a moment
where I am not holding the world up
with hands that haven't stopped shaking.
Because I am tired
of being the pillar.
Tired
of being the prayer,
never the answer.

SALT LINES

Tired
of being the ocean
when no one remembers
how much salt it takes
for someone to float.
I'm trying.
God, I'm trying.
Even when trying
feels like swallowing glass
and calling it nourishment.
If anyone asks,
tell them I loved too hard.
If anyone asks,
tell them I gave more than I had.
If anyone asks,
tell them I held on
longer than I should have
because hope,
however splintered,
was the only thing that ever felt like home.
And if I let go,
even if for just for a breath,
know that I did not give up.
I just needed
someone
to pour into me
for once.

PERENNIAL

PEOPLE COME AND GO
    like seasons,
    though no calendar marks their arrival.
    Some bloom in quietly,
    like spring
    whispers its way into the bones
    of those who have forgotten warmth
    during a frigid winter.
    They come with color,
    with a sense of maybe,
    with words that sound like beginnings.
    You let them in.
    How could you not?
    The winter has lasted so long,
    even a thaw can feel like God.
    Others burn in,

SALT LINES

like August.
Loud. Immediate.
They promise permanence
with every laugh
but leave behind
only scorched earth and fading echoes.
There are those who fall into your life
like October,
brilliant, beautiful,
yet dying from the start.
And some disappear like December mornings,
without a word,
just frost on the glass
where their breath used to be.
I used to hold spring in my fists.
I used to beg summer not to leave.
I used to tape the leaves
back onto the trees
as they fell in rust and regret.
The constellations change
with the tilt of the night sky.
What no one tells you
is how many versions of yourself
you'll shed
trying to be enough.
Or how you'll learn
that storms are scripture.
The kind of faith born

not from doctrine,
but from surviving
what others don't see.
I have held temples in my chest
and felt them become tombs.
I have been
the empty house
left abandoned
after being called home.
My walls still etched
with names no longer spoken.
They call it emotional instability
like it's a fault in the wiring.
What happens, then,
when we are too aware
of how temporary everything is?
What if we feel seasons deeper
because we've lived too many in a moment?
I am all of them at once.
The frostbite and the flame,
the thunder and the bloom.
I change like the weather,
but not without pattern.
The sacred texts I follow
are written
in wind,
in fireflies,
in the silence that follows

after someone forgets to say goodbye.

Truth doesn't wear one face.

That faith can be found

in the leaving,

not just the staying.

That even those who hurt you

might still have been holy

in the moment

they helped you breathe again.

People come and go.

Not all departures are betrayals.

Some are blessings disguised as goodbyes.

And maybe I am not meant

to keep anyone.

Maybe I am perennial.

Maybe I am

the change

they needed

before their own growth

could begin.

And maybe

that is enough.

THE SHEEP THAT WORE INK

I WAS BORN THE wrong hue
in a pasture of pastels.
Too jagged
for their lullabies.
Too tender
for their thunder.
A question mark
in a family
that only spoke in periods.
I laughed too hard.
I loved too much.
I lingered in thoughts too long
for their comfort.
From the start,

I was the one
they couldn't place.
The echo
that didn't match
the voice.
They called me different
like a diagnosis.
I asked
why the sky wept
on sunny days.
They said I was moody,
like I needed to be ashamed.
I danced
in rain puddles
no one else could see.
I was the side effect.
The page they skipped
I broke bread
with gods
they didn't believe in
and prayed
with my eyes open.
I stitched my soul together
from every altar,
and still
they said I was lost.
I learned to mold myself early.
I folded my fire

into their boxes.
I rewrote my voice
in their dialect.
I memorized the rules
of belonging.
I stayed quiet
when I should've screamed.
I smiled
when I should've shattered.
I was the peacekeeper
in wars I didn't start.
I was the mediator
in my own execution.
Still, they found fault.
Still, I was too much.
Still, I was too honest.
Still, I was too raw.
Still I was too inconvenient
when they preferred empathy prepackaged.
And when I stopped performing
and stepped off their stage,
I became the villain.
The problem child.
The walking mirror
they smashed
because it showed them
who they really were.
Every group,

every circle,
every so-called "chosen family"
that promised a place for me
until they realized I wouldn't
bleach my wool
to match their porcelain pride.
I've been the black sheep
in every flock I've entered,
not because I wander,
but because I refuse to be herded.
I stopped chasing validation.
I became their cautionary tale.
The punchline.
The problem.
The plot twist
they never saw coming.
But I am not their villain.
I am the unwritten chapter
they never dared read.
I am the question
their doctrines couldn't answer.
I am the holy
in ways they'll never see.
I am a prophet
with trembling hands.
They say I'm unstable.
I say I'm alive.
Divinity doesn't come

in one shape,

one faith,

one bloodline.

My soul is a tapestry

stitched with chaos and calm.

The tides rise within me

sometimes thunder,

sometimes sunny days,

but always truth.

Always me.

I've worn the name black sheep

like a armor and accusation.

I am the sheep

who carved his story in ink

when no one else would.

Here I stand,

half prayer,

half scar,

all heart.

I am proof misfits live,

where silence is sacred,

and where the sheep wear ink.

I was meant to awaken

every soul

still pretending .

I am the depth.

I am the spectrum.

I am the unseen strength.

Because being different
is never the curse.
It is the calling.

WHERE THE OCEAN
ALMOST KEPT ME

BORN WITH BRINE IN my blood,
    raised by salt-stung winds
    and lullabies sung in crashing waves.
    The ocean isn't a mystery,
    it's a memory,
    etched into my sunburnt shoulders
    and the rhythm of tides.
    But even old friends
    can turn on you.
    Even sacred places
    can become tombs.
    The rip.
    The reach.
    The choice.

SALT LINES

I saw someone slipping
and I dove before thinking,
because grief teaches you
how to bargain with your own body
to stop someone else from vanishing.
The water welcomed me,
then pulled me down
like it remembered something I didn't.
Like it knew
how many versions of me
wanted to disappear.
I fought.
Then I listened
to the quiet beneath the surface,
to the ache behind my eyes,
to the thought
that maybe this was easier
than staying broken
on land.
Not shouted,
not screamed,
just a whisper
that pierced the silence
like scripture in a dying man's ear:
"Keep going."
And the sea paused.
Like it, too, believed in her.
I kicked.

Not to escape.

To return

to the parts of me

still tethered to the world

by laughter I hadn't heard yet,

and situations where hands still needed holding.

The truth is

part of me never left

the salty grave.

Because now,

even in sleep,

I drown again.

Not in water,

but in memory.

In the feel of the pull.

In the voice that saved me.

In the question that still echoes:

Why was I spared again?

They say I'm brave.

I say I'm haunted.

Because when you've tasted death

and spat it back out,

you never stop tasting salt.

There's a church in me

where all my versions sit.

The loud one,

the laughing one,

the tired one,

the one that stared into the deep

and thought it looked like home.

They argue in languages

not even I understand.

One calls it courage.

Another calls it luck.

The quietest one

just hums

until I fall asleep again.

You can see it

if you watched how I flinch

at sudden joy.

In how I cry

at the kindness

I don't feel I deserve.

I was never built for evenness.

My mind runs in rip currents

pulling fast,

pulling deep,

pulling hard.

The current has a pattern

when chaos repeats itself

like a song sung by uncertain gods.

Faith in all things

and none of them.

Because I've seen the divine

in a voice,

in a gasp,

in the grip of a hand

that wouldn't let go.

I know now

waves don't push you down

because they're cruel.

They push you down

because sometimes

they see what the land does not.

The ache in your smile,

the cracks beneath your kindness,

the galaxies

fighting for air

between your ribs.

But I swam back.

And I keep swimming.

And some days,

that's the closest thing to a miracle

I'll ever believe in.

If I close my eyes tonight

and see water,

if I feel the pull again,

I'll whisper back

what I once heard in the deep.

"Keep going."

I am not a man

who drowned.

I am a man

who returned.

And the ocean.

She knows me still.

But now,

I know myself too.

JUST... DIFFERENT

THEY NEVER MEAN IT cruelly,
not always, anyway.
Just... different.
A phrase folded gently in tone,
but jagged in shape.
It cuts all the same.
Just... different
like my laughter
lasted too long
and was uncomfortable.
Just... different
like I loved too hard,
worked too late,
believed too much.
Just... different
like I cared past the point

where caring was normal

for anyone else.

Classrooms, boardrooms,

in break rooms and bedrooms

I carry it like a second spine.

Strong, but always aching.

Just... different.

A warning label

people read

before they get too close.

Caution: unpredictable tides.

They don't say "less than."

They say "unique."

They mean "unrelatable."

Just... different.

An outlier in every group hug,

the echo that didn't quite match the call.

Even in excellence,

my difference drew blood.

Work harder, they said.

So I did.

Better than most.

But even that becomes an exile.

Shining bright

Still invisible.

A dance between summer and winter,

between staying silent

and explaining the chaos of my universe.

It's not a black hole.
It's a galaxy,
just one they haven't mapped yet.
Some days, I am a water puddle,
reflecting the light in ways
the world never knew they needed.
Some days, I am the mirror
you didn't want to see yourself in.
And some days, I'm just... tired
of justifying the weather.
Just... different.
Like I haven't spent lifetimes
trying to translate my storm
into sunshine.
But I've heard the voices
of my inner pantheon.
Each one a god
in their own domain.
Calls for stillness,
For fire,
For silence,
For love that could flood cities.
I've learned to listen to them all,
without surrendering to any.
They don't see
my difference isn't anarchy,
it's democracy.
I've sat at the feet of every judge,

read the scriptures of sunrises,

whispered silent prayers loudly.

I've found fragments

in the grind of healing,

not in questioning.

I am a believer for survival,

believing because I must,

because to not believe

would mean I was made

to be mocked by the voices.

Just... different.

To love deeper,

to feel closer,

to question harder.

Just... different.

I survive what others would drown in.

I'm

Intense.

Too much.

Not enough.

Unsettling.

Brilliant.

Just... different.

I carry whole universes

in the gap between my lungs.

I still shine,

not despite it,

because of it.

Just... different.
My soul was not built
for fitting in.
It was built
for breaking molds.
To light the torches in rooms
no one ever thought to visit.
Just... different.
Never say
I wasn't authentic
when everyone else
chose a mask.
I was
Just... different.

UNSEEN, UNHEARD

WHISPERS LOST IN THE blowing wind,
 unheard and unseen,
 Hollowed out faces hidden amongst the shadows,
 absent from the dream.
 They move through the grounds,
 feeling nonexistent in their safe space,
 Their stories slowly erased,
 leaving them without a trace.
 What does it mean
 to be unseen, unheard?
 To be written out of history,
 as if they were never heard?
 To plant seeds in soil
 that never even knew their name,
 Their every essence buried
 beneath the same ol' blame.

They are surviving in a world
where their stories go untold,
Where the vibrance is dampened,
where the warmth grows cold.
Where voices once alive, bold, and free,
Are suddenly shrouded in darkness,
stripped of their natural right to be.
But alas they have an art beat
where words have failed,
In careful brushes of paint,
in soulful lyrics,
in unwritten tales all is unveiled.
They craft their resistance,
stroke by stroke,
In evocative poetry,
in fluid dance,
in the lost language of the hush.
Each line part of the resistance,
each stanza a slow, silent scream,
A watercolor painting of their souls,
masked inside a dream.
Their art speaks for them
when their voices cannot,
Exposing their hidden truth,
unshackled and hot.
They are not alone,
no matter how distant they may feel,
Together, our shared voices

weave their song's lyrics too loud to conceal.

Through the rhythm of the unheard,

together we will stand,

Our souls knot together

while the power is in their hand.

We gather not as one,

but as many and all,

Our stories script together,

refusing to fall.

With mind and body joined in peace,

we claim their right,

To be felt,

to be heard,

to shine in their own light.

Let their art hang in in the halls for all to see,

so bright and bold,

Let the truth we are hand-building

shatter the mold.

For in the sweet sound

of every key, pen, brush, and voice,

Together we declare loudly and proudly,

this is our first and final choice.

For them to no longer be sidelined,

cast to the fringe,

We rise together,

we speak together,

nothing on the fragile hinge.

Representation of all matters

in every space we tread,

It's not just a want;

it's the life they've led.

Unseen, unheard,

but they are more than this,

Bearing the weight

of what prior generations missed.

But no longer will they stand

outside of our view,

Through their art,

we highlight their stories through.

They are here, alive, full of vibrant hues,

We are all culture,

we are all history,

we are all the news.

Let them listen,

let them see,

The power of representation

in the strength of "we."

Join us now,

add your voice to the melodic songs,

For the path to equality

is where this campus belongs.

In each piece of their art crafted,

in every story they told,

We rise in unity,

commanding and bold.

Unseen, unheard,

but not for long,

They are the future,

their voices are strong.

AFTER I FORGOT MY NAME

I DRANK TO QUIET the room,

then the room learned to speak my language.

It asked for more.

So, I gave it more.

Night after night, I poured myself smaller

until the glass could hold me.

I told the mirror I was fine.

The mirror nodded,

then turned into a door I could not open.

I started measuring days

by how many lies fit in my mouth.

Work. Family. Friends.

I loved them all,

but the bottle got the first hello

and the last goodnight.
Some mornings the sun climbed the blinds
like it wanted me alive.
I pulled the cord
and asked it to come back later.
Later never came.
I learned the math of forgetting.
Two drinks made me kind.
Four made me brave.
Six erased the brakes.
After that, I was a rumor
wearing my own clothes.
I called it stress.
I called it culture.
I called it celebration.
Truth sat across the room,
counting what I would not count.
I prayed with a dry mouth.
Please let me be someone else.
Please let me be anyone else.
The answer was silence,
and the silence sounded like thirst.
There is a moment people miss
when they talk about bottoms.
It is not a crash.
It is a room with no corners,
only a slow circle where you keep meeting yourself
and each time you are less.

The phone rang.

I almost did not pick up.

A voice said, Try again.

Another said, I will sit with you.

No thunder.

Only a chair pulled close.

I put the bottle down.

My hand shook like it had a memory of staying.

I left the room.

The room followed me for weeks.

Sometimes it still does.

I learned how to count by breathing.

Four in.

Hold for four.

Four out.

Repeat until morning looks like a place I belong.

Coffee replaced rituals

I could no longer afford.

Water taught my bones a new prayer.

Walks became proof.

Left foot. Right foot.

I am still here.

I told the truth to one person.

Then two.

The third time I told it,

I heard my voice coming back with less echo.

Shame hates company.

I invited mine to sit and listen.

SALT LINES

I wrote names.

Some needed calls.

Some needed silence.

I made amends where the bridge still stood.

Where it was ash,

I buried a letter in the dirt

and promised the ground I would do no more harm.

I cleaned the kitchen at night.

Not for guests.

For the morning version of me

who always felt like a stranger.

I wanted him to see a place set for him.

I wanted him to stay.

I found myself in small rooms where nothing fancy happens.

A circle of chairs.

A phrase on a wall.

A cup of something warm.

People said their names like they were learning them again.

I said mine,

and it filled my mouth like first water.

I learned the shape of surrender.

It is not kneeling.

It is unclenching.

It is letting go of the story where I must lose.

I kept a photo from before.

I do not look away from him anymore.

He is not a warning.

He is a map of how much light it took to get here.

The cravings came like weather.
I checked the forecast,
not for a reason to be afraid,
but to pack what I needed.
Call a friend.
Eat real food.
Go outside.
Do any kind thing
that proves I still choose life.
I forgave the body that carried me drunk.
I forgave the mind that lied to survive.
I forgave the mouth that drank alone
because it did not know another way to speak.
I thanked the hands that now hold water,
pens,
dogs,
steering wheels at noon,
and doors for people walking behind me.
I am learning the difference
between who I was,
who I am,
and who I want to be.
It is a quiet hallway.
Each door opens when I knock softly.
Who I was thought relief was a liquid.
Who I am knows relief is a practice.
Who I want to be keeps the porch light on
for the days that run late.

SALT LINES

He knows I will arrive,

even if I stop to cry in the car.

I do not chase perfection.

I stack small good things

until they are taller than the bad hour.

Sleep.

Food.

Phone a friend.

Write three lines of something true.

Pet the dog twice.

Pet the dog a third time

because he deserves it.

I stopped asking the past to teach me new tricks.

It only knows one.

Instead, I let the present show me where to stand.

On grass.

On kitchen tile.

On a sidewalk I can sweep when it is mine.

Some days I miss the noise.

I name the feeling.

Lonely.

Restless.

Hungry for an old lie.

Then I feed myself something honest

until the hunger remembers a better name.

I keep a list of proofs.

Today I tasted strawberries.

Today I called my mother back.

Today I returned the cart to its home.
Today I told someone no,
and the world did not end.
I do not worship pain anymore.
It is not a god.
It is a weather report.
I keep a jacket near the door.
I keep walking.
If you look at me now,
you might still see yesterday's smoke.
That is fine.
Fire taught me heat.
Water taught me breath.
Time taught me the length of a day
is exactly long enough.
I want to be a person who arrives.
To appointments.
To friendships.
To his own life.
I want to be a person who leaves
when leaving is the kindest choice.
For me.
For you.
For the man in the mirror
who finally answers when I ask his name.
I end the night with water on the table
and a promise I can keep.
Sleep, and we will try again.

SALT LINES

Morning, and we will try again.

If noon breaks me,

I will try again at one.

I am not cured.

I am committed.

I am not finished.

I am in motion.

I am not a ghost.

I am a man who stands where he can be found.

If you ask what I am now,

I will not say sober like it is a medal.

I will say present,

which is the only door that opens from both sides.

If you ask who I want to be,

I will say someone my younger self would sit with.

Someone my older self will trust with the keys.

Someone who remembers how heavy a glass can be

and how light a life begins to feel

when you set it down

and pick yourself up

with both hands.

"

HE

I USED TO SAY I was alone.

    The room agreed.

    Silence did most of the talking.

    I waited for family to find me.

    No one knocked.

    So I learned to build a table.

    Two chairs at first.

    Then three.

    A fourth for the day I might be brave.

    I made coffee for strangers

    who were only strangers once.

    I learned names slow,

    like learning a song by ear.

    We took turns telling the truth.

    We passed the sugar.

    We passed the time.

SALT LINES

We kept passing until it felt like keeping.

I set aside a plate for the latecomer.

Sometimes the latecomer was me.

They did not ask me to explain.

They asked if I would sit.

I used to think my heart was missing.

It was only buried.

I found it under old stories

that said strength means quiet,

that said help is for someone else.

I brushed off the dirt.

It beat like it had somewhere to be.

I watered it with small acts.

Return the text.

Call back.

Hold the door.

Tell the waiter the soup was good.

Tell the friend you were wrong.

Tell yourself you can try again at one.

The heart learned new work.

It carried groceries and grief.

It kept time at funerals.

It laughed out loud in kitchens.

It gave rides to the airport at 5 a.m.

It forgave the body for what it once needed.

It forgave the mind for calling that need love.

I thought knowledge was something you take.

A book.

A rule.

A badge that proves you were right.

Then I tried to teach what I knew.

Suddenly I knew less

and learned more.

I learned by showing my hands.

Here is the scar.

Here is the stitch.

Here is the tool that worked on Tuesday

and failed on Wednesday.

Here is how I hold myself steady

without a promise that today will be easy.

I taught what kept me breathing.

Make a list.

Eat real food.

Move your body once an hour.

Tell the truth before it grows teeth.

Say no without a reason.

Say yes with both feet.

Students appeared that were never students.

A neighbor at the mailbox.

A voice from a meeting I almost skipped.

A friend's kid in the back seat

asking why the sky looks closer at night.

I said, Because we are,

and left it at that.

Family changed shape.

It looked less like blood

and more like practice.

It sounded like key rings

and group chats.

It smelled like coffee at six,

like soup when money is thin,

like laundry because someone remembered.

We marked holidays with who showed up.

We made new ones when the old ones hurt.

First Day the Heat Came On.

Cherry Season.

The night we all sat on the floor

because the furniture was too far away.

I grew a heart that could stay.

It did not win arguments.

It did not keep score.

It kept time.

Breathe in four.

Hold four.

Out four.

Again.

Again.

Again.

I stopped looking for a door

that swings only one way.

I opened windows.

I learned the light by its weight on my cheek.

I learned the dark by listening

without reaching for a switch.

Some days I forget I am allowed to be here.

On those days I teach the class again.

Lesson one, you are not late.

Lesson two, you can start now.

Lesson three, start small.

When I falter, I count proofs.

Today I folded the towel.

Today I fed the dog first.

Today I wrote three lines

and did not delete them.

Today I told a story that ended with hope

and meant it.

I keep a chair open at the table.

I keep a light on near the sink.

I keep a pen where I can find it.

I keep a promise simple enough to keep.

Sleep, and we try again.

Wake, and we try again.

Break, and we try again when the hands are free.

If you ask me what I know,

I will point to what I share.

If you ask me where my heart is,

I will point to who I call.

If you ask me who my family is,

I will point to the table,

to the extra chair,

to the door that stays unlocked

for the friend who finally knocks.

Hallowed Spirits

I have seen holy people.
  Not because of robes.
  Because they showed up at noon
  with hands that shook
  and still held on.
  We called them spirits
  because they survived so much wind.
  They took their seats in small rooms.
  They spoke in first names.
  They poured coffee like prayer.
  Life was on the fritz.
  Phones full of apologies.
  Bank accounts thin.
  Bodies tired from the miles between beds.
  Minds loud with a chorus of old choices.
  A new challenge kept arriving.

It did not knock.

It showed up like weather.

Hot.

Cold.

Too much.

Too fast.

We learned to pack for it.

Call a friend.

Eat real food.

Drink water.

Walk to the corner and back.

Repeat until the room feels bigger.

We lit rooms with simple light.

We told the truth in small portions.

We listened until the story lost its teeth.

We let silence sit with us

without picking a fight.

I saw people practice surrender

and keep their dignity.

They took the bottle's crown

and set it on the table.

They bowed their heads, not in defeat,

but to hear their own heart better.

Something must die, someone said,

before everything breaks.

Let the lie die.

Let the fantasy die.

Let the story where you always lose

stop breathing first.

Death before destruction.

We wrote it on a scrap and folded it twice.

We kept it in a pocket

with the names we could call.

We touched it when the old music played.

We carried losses like honest weight.

We did not turn them into museums.

We turned them into maps.

This corner is dangerous.

This store has a smell that lies.

This number on my phone is a trap.

Choose another street.

Delete what does not wish me well.

The challenge kept changing clothes.

Lonely at lunch.

Restless at ten.

Angry at nothing around three.

We learned to check our hunger by name.

Hungry.

Angry.

Lonely.

Tired.

We fed each one the right meal.

Soup for the body.

Phone for the heart.

Quiet for the mind.

Sleep for the rest of me.

We kept new holidays.

First morning with clear eyes.

The day a laugh did not sound borrowed.

The night the mirror nodded back

without asking questions I could not answer.

I watched the bravest lesson.

How to stay.

Stay in the hard chair.

Stay through the craving.

Stay until the calendar earns a new page.

We did not become saints.

We learned our sizes.

We wore days that fit.

We hemmed our hours with routine.

Keys in the bowl.

Shoes by the door.

Phone on do not disturb after nine.

We paid old debts one honest dollar at a time.

We wrote letters we would never mail

because the bridge was ash.

We apologized where the bridge still stood.

We did not ask for parades.

We asked for a chance to do better twice.

The body remembered how to trust me.

It let me sleep.

It let my hands carry groceries

instead of shame.

It let my feet get tired for good reasons.

SALT LINES

Stairs.

Parks.

Dancing in kitchens with nobody watching.

The mind learned new work.

Not to solve.

To notice.

A thought is a cloud.

A craving is a wave.

Both pass if I keep my feet on the floor.

We found teachers everywhere.

A neighbor who waters plants at dawn.

A child who asks why the moon follows us.

A cashier who says see you tomorrow

like a contract I want to keep.

We taught what kept us breathing.

Make the bed for the person you will be at night.

Leave water by the lamp.

Say no like a sentence.

Say yes like a promise with a date.

The old room still calls sometimes.

It offers a chair with a view of nothing.

I tell it I have another place to be.

A table with names.

A light by the sink.

A door that opens from both sides.

Growth came quiet.

No trumpet.

Only shirts that smelled like soap.

Plants that did not die.

A calendar with more ink than excuses.

Life after growth looks like this.

Keys that fit.

Meals that include greens.

Walks that start without bargaining.

Mornings that arrive on time

and find me there.

I do not worship suffering now.

I let it knock.

I open the door with my jacket on.

I say you can sit,

but you cannot drive.

Then I text a friend

and we talk about nothing until it leaves.

I keep the scrap of paper.

Death before destruction.

I read it when I forget which comes first.

Let the old lie die

so the house does not burn.

Then I read the other note.

Life after growth.

I tuck it in the mirror frame.

It reminds me to water the plant.

It reminds me to write three lines.

It reminds me to keep the extra chair open.

If you ask me what is holy,

I will point to a room where people look up

when a latecomer enters.
If you ask me what is sacred,
I will point to a quiet noon
where someone pours coffee
and asks, will you sit.
We start again where we stand.
We keep the lights simple.
We keep our names plain.
We keep our promises small enough to carry.
I have seen holy people.
They are us.
We are still here.
We are learning how to stay.
We are learning how to grow first,
so life can follow.

Architect of the Universe

I PLANNED THE WRECK.

I drew the lines myself.

Rooms with no windows.

Stairs that went nowhere.

Locks on the inside.

Keys on the floor.

I picked the paint that would not dry.

I bought the nails that bent.

I stacked my days like unsafe bricks

and called it home because I was tired.

Architects of destruction.

That was the job title I gave myself.

Project manager of my own collapse.

Crew chief of every bad idea.

SALT LINES

We broke ground at midnight.
We worked weekends.
We left the site a mess.
People tried to name me.
Sinner.
Savior.
Problem.
Proof.
Healer when I poured coffee in small rooms
and kept a newcomer's hands busy.
Murderer when I counted the hurt I caused
and the hours that never come back.
Labeled healers, they said,
when I sat with someone at 2 a.m.
and told the truth without decoration.
Labeled murderers, they said,
when my silence cut deeper than any word
and my leaving left a crater.
I carried both names in the same pocket.
One scratched.
One burned.
Neither helped me sleep.
Called a blessing at birthday tables
by people who still believed in candles.
Felt cursed in bathrooms with the fan on
counting reasons to keep breathing.
This is the math of early mornings.
This is the arithmetic of shame.

I wanted a verdict that stayed put.

Guilty or good.

Instead I got a ledger.

Debits.

Credits.

Pay as you go.

I learned demolition first.

What to tear down.

Old lies.

Old numbers.

Old routes that always pass a bar.

Old songs that turn my hands into someone else's.

Death before destruction, I heard.

Let the lie die so the house does not burn.

So I killed a story.

I killed the throne I built for a bottle.

I let the king go without a parade.

The job changed.

We fenced the site.

We posted a permit that said repair.

We swept.

We sorted.

We kept what could carry weight.

We hauled the rest to the curb.

I called the inspectors.

A friend with three years.

A neighbor who knows grief by name.

A woman from the back row

who taught me how to breathe when my hands shook.

They did not sign with ink.

They signed with time.

Footings first.

Food on a schedule.

Water before coffee.

Sleep like a duty, not a prize.

Phone a friend at noon

even when I do not need to.

Especially then.

We framed the day with routines.

Make the bed.

Open the blinds.

Speak the truth

even if each one is short.

Say them out loud

to hear my own voice return.

I learned to measure progress in inches.

The plant did not die this month.

The cart went back to its home.

The dog went out on time.

The bill was paid before the red notice.

The laugh sounded like it belonged to me.

Labels kept trying to stick.

Healer.

Murderer.

Saint.

Wreckage.

I let them pass over me like weather.

Rain for a while.

Then sun on the steps.

Either way, the mail still runs.

Either way, the dishes need washing.

I showed up where chairs make circles.

I said my name like a person

and not a warning.

I listened to people who took their halos off

and put on work gloves.

They told me nobody floats to shore.

Everybody swims.

On anniversaries I do not post.

I sweep the porch.

I call the one who called me.

I take the picture down and look at it with both eyes.

I thank the man in the frame for surviving

long enough to make it heavy.

I make amends where the bridge still stands.

I step back from the rivers I cannot cross.

I write letters and burn them cold.

I pay for what I can without turning it into theater.

I let the rest be a vow with a date.

I keep a toolkit I can carry.

Breathing in fours.

HALT written on the fridge.

Hungry.

Angry.

SALT LINES

Lonely.

Tired.

Feed the right one.

Call the right name.

Sleep when the list grows teeth.

I build what stays.

A calendar with more ink than excuses.

A kitchen that looks ready in the morning.

Shoes by the door that still fit.

A voice that answers the phone and says yes

or no

without a story attached.

Some days the old hard hat calls to me.

Come back to the site where nothing stands.

Sit in the dust.

Remember how simple it felt to give up.

I tell it I have another job.

I point to the window I can unlock.

I point to the table with an extra chair.

I point to the light by the sink.

If you ask what I am now,

I will not hand you a title.

I will hand you a list of what I did today.

A list small enough to carry.

I kept my word at nine.

I ate when I should have.

I walked until the thought passed.

I told someone the truth before it hurt more.

If you want to name me,

call me a builder of mornings.

Call me a steward of keys.

Call me a neighbor who returns what he borrows.

Call me at noon when the room gets loud.

I will answer.

I still hear the old words across town.

Healer.

Murderer.

Blessing.

Curse.

I write them in a notebook

then turn the page.

There is more paper.

There is more day.

I keep blueprints that fit in a pocket.

Simple lines.

Enough walls for privacy.

Enough doors for air.

Rooms big enough for a circle of chairs.

A kitchen that never runs out of cups.

A porch light I leave on

for whoever is late.

Sometimes that is me.

I do not worship my past.

I thank it for the lesson

and send it home.

I do not trust my future with everything.

SALT LINES

I give it a sandwich and a plan.
I trust this hour.
This breath.
This small good thing.
Architects of destruction,
I know how to be that man.
I also know how to set my tools down
when they only build fires.
Today I choose a hammer that fixes.
Today I choose a level that tells the truth.
Today I choose my hands for holding,
not for breaking.
Called a blessing by someone who stayed because I did.
Felt cursed at three when the noise returned.
I let both be true for a minute.
Then I made tea.
Then I sent a text.
Then I put water by the bed
and wrote three lines.
We will try again.
If noon breaks me,
we will try again at one.
This is the work.
This is the building that does not collapse
when you live inside it.
This is the name I can answer
without looking down.

"Devil's Deal"

The dark still knows my number.

It calls by name.

It offers a shortcut.

It promises a headline I will not have to earn.

It says the work is over if I follow.

It speaks fast.

It flatters.

It tells me I am special.

It says the rules do not apply to me.

It says there is an easier life in the next room.

I have walked toward that voice.

I have paid at the door.

The price was hidden in small print.

Sleep first.

Friends next.

Health last.

At the end the receipt said everything.

Fortune and fame, the dark says.

It means applause from strangers.

It means silence at home.

It means bright lights at midnight.

It means a long walk back in the morning.

The dark says a better life.

It means a life I do not have to feel.

It means a life that skips the work.

It means a life that ends early.

It does not say that part out loud.

Death carries a calendar.

He does not rush.

He waits in chairs I used to choose.

He holds out a pen.

Sign here when you are tired.

I heard another voice once.

It was quiet.

It did not sell anything.

It said, breathe.

It said, call someone and say your name.

I started counting proofs instead of promises.

Four breaths in.

Hold four.

Four out.

Repeat until the hands stop shaking.

I made coffee.

I filled a glass with water.

I ate real food.

I put on shoes and walked to the corner.

I came back and wrote three lines of something true.

I checked my hunger by name.

Hungry.

Angry.

Lonely.

Tired.

I fed each the right thing.

A meal.

A talk.

A room with people in it.

A bed at a decent hour.

I cleaned the kitchen at night.

I left a cup by the sink.

I set the keys in the bowl.

I opened the blinds in the morning.

I let the light find me.

I sat in small rooms.

I listened to first names.

I passed the sugar.

I learned how to tell the truth in short sentences.

I learned how to sit still until a hard moment passed.

I put old numbers on a do not call list.

I turned down the songs that turn my feet the wrong way.

I took a different street home.

I learned which aisles lie.

I learned which hours are loud and made a plan for them.

I wrote a list for noon.

Drink water.

Eat a sandwich.

Text the one who texts back.

Walk five minutes.

Repeat if the room still spins.

I paid what I could.

I said I am sorry where it mattered.

I said it with actions that held.

I did not look for applause.

SALT LINES

I looked for a second chance to do better.

I kept a photo from before.

I do not look away.

He is not a warning.

He is a map of how far I have walked.

He is the reason I keep walking.

The dark still calls.

Sometimes I answer with silence.

Sometimes I answer with a schedule.

Food at twelve.

Walk at three.

Bed before ten.

Sometimes I answer with names.

I call the friend who picked up for me.

I leave the door open for the latecomer.

Sometimes the latecomer is me.

They save me a seat.

When the pitch gets loud, I read the facts.

Today I returned the cart.

Today I laughed without asking permission.

Today I told the truth before it hurt more.

Today I kept my word at nine.

I keep notes on the mirror.

Keep it simple.

Drink water first.

Say no like a sentence.

Say yes with both feet.

Leave the porch light on.

I am not special to the dark.

It calls everyone.

It is good at it.

I am not helpless either.

I keep a toolkit near the door.

Breathing.

Names I can call.

A chair in a circle.

Shoes for walking.

A list small enough to carry.

The dark offers a better life in exchange for what I cannot pay.

It wants the quiet that comes after a last breath.

I want the quiet that comes after a hard hour.

We do not agree on price.

So I hang up.

If the phone rings again, I will be ready.

Coffee on.

Water poured.

Keys in the bowl.

A chair at the table with my name on it.

I will sit.

I will stay.

I will live the day that is in front of me.

If noon breaks me, we try again at one.

This is how I keep what the dark cannot sell me.

This is how I keep myself.

DEVILS DEAL

THE DARK STILL KNOWS my number.

It calls by name.

It offers a shortcut.

It promises a headline I will not have to earn.

It says the work is over if I follow.

It speaks fast.

It flatters.

It tells me I am special.

It says the rules do not apply to me.

It says there is an easier life in the next room.

I have walked toward that voice.

I have paid at the door.

The price was hidden in small print.

Sleep first.

Friends next.

Health last.

At the end the receipt said everything.

Fortune and fame, the dark says.

It means applause from strangers.

It means silence at home.

It means bright lights at midnight.

It means a long walk back in the morning.

The dark says a better life.

It means a life I do not have to feel.

It means a life that skips the work.

It means a life that ends early.

It does not say that part out loud.

Death carries a calendar.

He does not rush.

He waits in chairs I used to choose.

He holds out a pen.

Sign here when you are tired.

I heard another voice once.

It was quiet.

It did not sell anything.

It said, breathe.

It said, call someone and say your name.

I started counting proofs instead of promises.

Four breaths in.

Hold four.

Four out.

Repeat until the hands stop shaking.

I made coffee.

I filled a glass with water.

SALT LINES

I ate real food.

I put on shoes and walked to the corner.

I came back and wrote three lines of something true.

I checked my hunger by name.

Hungry.

Angry.

Lonely.

Tired.

I fed each the right thing.

A meal.

A talk.

A room with people in it.

A bed at a decent hour.

I cleaned the kitchen at night.

I left a cup by the sink.

I set the keys in the bowl.

I opened the blinds in the morning.

I let the light find me.

I sat in small rooms.

I listened to first names.

I passed the sugar.

I learned how to tell the truth in short sentences.

I learned how to sit still until a hard moment passed.

I put old numbers on a do not call list.

I turned down the songs that turn my feet the wrong way.

I took a different street home.

I learned which aisles lie.

I learned which hours are loud and made a plan for them.

I wrote a list for noon.

Drink water.

Eat a sandwich.

Text the one who texts back.

Walk five minutes.

Repeat if the room still spins.

I paid what I could.

I said I am sorry where it mattered.

I said it with actions that held.

I did not look for applause.

I looked for a second chance to do better.

I kept a photo from before.

I do not look away.

He is not a warning.

He is a map of how far I have walked.

He is the reason I keep walking.

The dark still calls.

Sometimes I answer with silence.

Sometimes I answer with a schedule.

Food at twelve.

Walk at three.

Bed before ten.

Sometimes I answer with names.

I call the friend who picked up for me.

I leave the door open for the latecomer.

Sometimes the latecomer is me.

They save me a seat.

When the pitch gets loud, I read the facts.

Today I returned the cart.

Today I laughed without asking permission.

Today I told the truth before it hurt more.

Today I kept my word at nine.

I keep notes on the mirror.

Keep it simple.

Drink water first.

Say no like a sentence.

Say yes with both feet.

Leave the porch light on.

I am not special to the dark.

It calls everyone.

It is good at it.

I am not helpless either.

I keep a toolkit near the door.

Breathing.

Names I can call.

A chair in a circle.

Shoes for walking.

A list small enough to carry.

The dark offers a better life in exchange for what I cannot pay.

It wants the quiet that comes after a last breath.

I want the quiet that comes after a hard hour.

We do not agree on price.

So I hang up.

If the phone rings again, I will be ready.

Coffee on.

Water poured.

Keys in the bowl.

A chair at the table with my name on it.

I will sit.

I will stay.

I will live the day that is in front of me.

If noon breaks me, we try again at one.

This is how I keep what the dark cannot sell me.

This is how I keep myself.

SCORNED

I HAVE HUNG BY a thread.

Not a figure of speech.

A real small thing you cannot see,

that still holds.

Some nights the thread felt slick.

Memory slipped off it.

Names blurred.

The order of events went soft around the edges.

I woke up already apologizing.

I told myself it was fine.

It was not.

I kept moving so I would not have to look straight at it.

I called the blur stress.

I called the empty spots busy.

I called the ache a long day.

Pain came in a brand I could buy.

Manmade.

Shelf stable.

On sale at the end of the aisle that lies.

It promised variety.

It delivered the same result.

Numb first.

Noise later.

The bill at the end always said the same thing.

Everything.

Everything felt the same for a while.

Joy and panic wore one mask.

Morning and midnight shared a voice.

I forgot how to tell better from different.

I forgot how to stop.

Heat lived under my ribs.

A burn that argued for action.

Jump in, it said.

Jump into the noise.

Jump into the rush.

Jump anywhere that is not here.

I jumped into water instead.

Cold.

Ten breaths long.

I jumped into shoes and walked to the corner.

I jumped into a chair in a circle.

I jumped into a call before the thought could grow teeth.

I let the fire be weather.

I dressed for it.

I worked on the mind I used to let run the whole show.

Correct is the wrong word.

Steady is closer.

I named what was loud.

Hungry.

Angry.

Lonely.

Tired.

I answered each without drama.

Food.

Quiet.

Company.

Sleep.

See what you can find, I told myself.

Find the proof that today happened.

The cart went home.

The dog ate first.

The bill got paid before the red ink.

Three true lines made it onto paper.

I read them out loud so my voice would come back.

I learned rest is a skill.

For years I scorned it.

Sleep was a prize for perfect people.

I had not met any.

So I chased a moving finish line.

The body kept score.

Blood drummed in my ears at two a.m.

Thoughts marched.

I held the phone like a torch in a cave and made it worse.

I made bedtime a job.

Water on the table.

Screens off.

Room cool.

Breath in four.

Hold four.

Out four.

Repeat until morning finds me.

On nights the drum would not quiet,

I did not sign the old contract.

I got up.

I folded two towels slow.

I counted to one hundred without judging how long it took.

I wrote a list for the next hour, not the next life.

Sit.

Breathe.

Back to bed when ready.

Try again.

I stopped worshiping pain.

It is not holy.

It is a signal.

I let it ring.

Then I answered with actions, not stories.

I sat with people who do this work.

Small rooms.

Plain words.

Chairs that face each other.

We passed sugar.

We passed time.

We learned how to say our names like we mean to keep them.

We talked about threads.

The ones we almost let go.

The ones we braided into something that could hold weight.

No magic.

Just hands that keep showing up.

I cleaned the kitchen at night for the person I am in the morning.

I left the blinds open so the light could find me.

I put keys in the same bowl so I would not start the day with a search.

I kept the coffee quiet.

I drank water first.

I took another street to avoid the aisle that lies.

I turned down songs that make my hands forget me.

I put numbers on a do not call list.

I learned which hours are loud.

I stacked small plans at those times.

Walk at three.

Text at seven.

Bed before ten.

When shame tried to make a feast of my history,

I set a smaller table.

One plate.

One fork.

One next right thing.

I ate what I could and left the rest in the past where it belongs.

Some days I still hang by that thread.

So I keep both hands free.

I do not fill them with arguments.

I do not carry more than I can hold.

I keep a pocket for simple tools.

Breathing.

Water.

Names I can call.

Steps I can take until the thought passes.

I made amends where the bridge still stands.

I did not perform.

I took my place in the line of people who are sorry and mean it.

I paid what I could.

I kept paying with new behavior when money was not the thing.

I keep a photo from before in a place I can reach.

I do not look away.

He is not a warning.

He is a measure of distance.

He proves the thread has held longer than I thought.

I teach what helps me stay.

Make the bed for the person you will be at night.

Leave a light near the sink.

Say no like a full sentence.

Say yes with both feet.

Tell the truth before it grows teeth.

On good days I forget to count.

On hard days I count on purpose.

Four in.

Hold.

Four out.

Again.

Again.

Until numbers turn into quiet.

It is simple, not easy.

It is ordinary, which is the point.

Ordinary life is the better life I thought I could buy.

I earn it by being here when it starts.

If the thread thins, I call.

If the call fails, I knock.

If the door stays shut, I sit where I am and breathe until the room gets bigger.

I do not leave myself unsupervised with a bad hour.

I am learning to rest without scorn.

To let the drum slow.

To let the body be a place that does not need to be punished to be trusted.

To let my mind stop sprinting long enough to hear a softer plan.

I keep a ledger of small proofs.

Today I was on time.

Today I did not raise my voice at a person who did not deserve it.

Today I ate food that came on a plate and had color.

Today I returned what I borrowed.

Today I laughed and it sounded like me.

I do not claim victory.

I keep a practice.

Break, and try again when the hands are free.

Hanging on by a thread can be enough.

Not forever.

For now.

For the length of a breath.

For the distance from the chair to the door and back.

For the space between a promise and the keeping of it.

What I find, when I look, is not secret.

It is a cup of water.

A name on my phone.

A room with chairs in a circle.

A morning that arrives on time and finds me ready.

Pain is not my planner.

The past is not my landlord.

The thread is not the whole story.

It is how I stay while I build the rest.

I am here.

I am steady enough for today.

If noon breaks me, I will try again at one.

If memory flees, I will write the truth down and read it back.

If the burn returns, I will dress for the weather and step outside.

I will keep the thread where I can feel it.

I will keep both hands free.

I will keep the light near the sink.

I will keep going.

One breath.

One small good thing.

Again.

LABYRINTH

THE FAMILY I BUILT is real.

The friends I made still answer.

The hand I was dealt is not the only one I play.

Yet some days the pictures smudge.

Names thin.

Moments lose their edges.

Memory steps back like it forgot the address.

I ask it to stay.

It drifts.

I call it louder.

It fades polite.

I stand in the kitchen with the light on

and try again.

Helpless comes easy when the noise gets bold.

Stop, I say.

The thought ignores me.

Another thought pops.

Then three more.

They crowd the doorway and act like they live here.

I forget what I was doing.

I remember only the ache.

I used to reach for manmade quiet.

It worked for a minute.

Then every feeling wore one mask.

Happy. Fear. Shame. Pride.

Same face.

Same trick.

Same bill at the end.

The path inside me turns.

Left, then left again.

Dim halls.

Familiar walls.

Slight burns where old choices touched skin.

A thousand flaws like pushpins in a map.

All the places I have been unkind to myself.

I do not fix a maze by running faster.

I slow down.

Left hand on the wall.

Breath in four.

Hold four.

Out four.

I keep my feet honest until the room gets wider.

I call what is loud by name.

Hungry.

SALT LINES

Angry.

Lonely.

Tired.

I feed each the right thing.

Food that is food.

Quiet without a screen.

A voice that knows my middle name.

Sleep I do not have to earn.

I keep proof I was here.

Coffee mug rinsed.

Keys in the bowl.

Sink light on for morning.

Three true lines on a page I will read out loud.

Return the cart.

Water the plant.

Pet the dog twice.

A third time for good measure.

I sit where chairs make a circle.

I say my name like I intend to keep it.

I listen to people who have learned to stay.

We pass sugar.

We pass the hour.

We tell the truth in short sentences.

We do not fix each other.

We sit close enough that fixing is not the only plan.

I carry a photo from before.

I look at it with both eyes.

He is not a warning.

He is a measure.

He proves the road is real because I have walked it.

When the fog thickens, I write a smaller list.

Drink water.

Eat something with color.

Walk to the corner.

Text the one who texts back.

If the hands shake, count to thirty and call.

If the call fails, sit and breathe until the room returns.

I practice rest.

I used to scorn it.

Now I set it like a table.

Dark room.

Cool air.

Phone facedown.

A cup within reach.

Breath like a metronome the body can trust.

Some nights the drum in my blood will not quit.

I do not sign the old contract.

I fold two towels.

I thank the body for telling the truth out loud.

Back to bed when ready.

Sleep is not a prize.

It is a tool.

I make amends where the bridge still stands.

I repair with hands, not speeches.

Where the bridge is gone, I write a letter and let it rest.

I stop building museums to my mistakes.

SALT LINES

I build mornings instead.

Family does not forget me when memory blurs.

They ask if I will sit.

Friends keep a chair free when I am late.

Sometimes the latecomer is me.

They pour coffee like a promise kept.

I still have turns I do not love.

I still see walls that remember my worst.

I still feel the singe of an old flame close by.

I count flaws without letting them vote.

They live here.

They do not lead.

I keep the map simple.

Take the bright street.

Skip the aisle that lies.

Turn down the song that makes my hands forget me.

Choose the door that opens from both sides.

If noon breaks me, I try again at one.

If memory slips, I read my lines out loud.

If the noise starts selling miracles, I check the price.

I have paid it before.

I am not paying again.

The family I built is proof I can build.

The friends I made are proof I can stay.

The hand I was dealt is only the first chapter.

The rest is work I can do with a steady breath.

Light by the sink.

Keys in the bowl.

A table with an extra chair.

Sleep, and we try again.

Wake, and we try again.

Break, and we try again when the hands are free.

The maze is still a maze.

I am no longer lost.

I am the one with the small flashlight,

the simple plan,

and enough quiet to hear my own feet find the way.

LE FEY

STRONG TIES, STRONG LIES.

   I wore both.

   Strings I called loyalty.

   Stories I called truth.

   They held tight.

   They pulled me the wrong way.

   I tied myself to old rooms.

   To bottles with pet names.

   To people who loved my mask.

   To a schedule that only worked at midnight.

   The knot looked neat.

   The life did not.

   The tongue knows tricks.

   It can bless and break in the same breath.

   It said one more will help.

   It said you earned it.

It said nobody understands.

It said you are the exception.

The wicked sung.

A chorus of easy answers.

The song had a hook I could not stop humming.

I turned it down.

It got louder.

I turned it off.

It moved into my head and kept time with my pulse.

I needed new music.

Quiet first.

Breath next.

Four in.

Hold four.

Four out.

Repeat until the room hears me.

I went looking for light that does not brag.

A thousand fireflies.

Tiny, steady.

They did not sell anything.

They blinked yes, then rested.

They asked me to do the same.

I made a list of small lights.

Keys in the bowl.

Dishes rinsed.

Text returned.

Dog walked before I thought too much.

Water before coffee.

SALT LINES

Three true lines on paper I can read out loud.

The prize was unassuming.

Not a medal.

Not applause.

A morning I belong to.

A laugh that sounds like it was born at home.

A bed that welcomes me because I kept my word.

I stopped asking the old knot to hold.

I learned new ties.

Phone a friend at noon.

Sit in a circle with chairs.

Say my name like I mean to keep it.

Pass sugar.

Pass the hour.

Pass the truth around the table.

There are days to act hard.

Take the bull by the horns, they say.

Some fights need a firm grip.

Some thoughts need a firm no.

Some calls need a hang up.

Be careful of his thorns.

Power cuts if you grab without thinking.

I put on gloves made of habits that last.

Food on time.

Sleep like a duty.

Shoes by the door.

Routes that skip the aisle that lies.

Songs that keep my hands mine.

I learned the names of traps.

Hungry.

Angry.

Lonely.

Tired.

I feed what needs feeding.

I walk when the room is small.

I call when the story grows teeth.

I cleaned the kitchen for the person I am at dawn.

I left a cup by the sink.

I opened the blinds so the light could find me.

I kept proof I was here when memory goes thin.

A note on the mirror that says drink water first.

Another that says say no like a sentence.

I made amends where the bridge still stands.

I used hands, not speeches.

Where the bridge is gone, I wrote a letter and let it rest.

I stopped building museums to my worst day.

I built mornings instead.

The tongue still tries to turn me.

I answer with action.

Return the cart.

Pet the dog twice.

A third time because he waits for me.

Tell the friend I was wrong.

Tell myself I can start now.

Fireflies keep their pace.

Blink. Rest.

SALT LINES

Yes. Pause.

I practice that rhythm.

Work, then water.

Noise, then breath.

Company, then quiet.

Some knots slip on wet days.

I watch without panic.

I add another tie.

I stay where my feet are.

I let help hold the weight my pride cannot.

Strong ties, strong lies.

I choose ties that keep me.

I leave lies on the shelf that sells them.

Wicked tongue, the wicked sung.

I keep my mouth for truth in short sentences.

I borrow a quieter song from people who show up.

A thousand fireflies, an unassuming prize.

I count them at night when the pitch starts.

I count them in the morning when I would rather forget.

Take the bull by the horns when I must.

Be careful of his thorns every time.

Grip with purpose.

Let go on time.

Wash the cut.

Call a friend.

Mark the lesson, not the scar.

If noon breaks me, I try again at one.

If the song returns, I turn up the lights I can move.

If the knot loosens, I tie it again with both hands steady.

Sleep, and we try again.

Wake, and we try again.

Live simple, and let the small lights lead me home.

CHALICE

WHAT CAN YOU DO

when your heart does not fit

in the hands that promise to heal it.

When their grip is small

and your pulse keeps spilling over the edge.

You try to fold yourself down.

You try to make less noise.

You try to say thank you

for a chair that pinches.

You pretend the ache is gratitude.

It is not.

Some rooms love the select few.

They speak in passwords.

They smile with their teeth and guard the door.

They call it care.

It feels like a test.

They dig holes for the ones who do not fit.

They call the digging bold.

You know a grave when you see one.

You sit in the quiet pew at the side.

You watch the light find dust and call it holy.

You do not sing.

You swallow once.

A cup flashes gold in your mind.

It says the old promise.

Easy.

Warm.

No questions asked.

The price comes later.

The receipt reads everything.

What can you do.

You start with breath.

Four in.

Hold four.

Four out.

Repeat until the noise stops shouting.

You pick a seat where chairs make a circle.

No altar.

No throne.

A coffee pot that burns a little.

A sugar bowl with a spoon that has seen things.

First names only.

Truth in short sentences.

Hands that shake and still pour.

SALT LINES

You build a bigger bowl for your own heart.

Food on time.

Water before coffee.

Sleep like a duty, not a prize.

Walk to the corner.

Come back.

Write three lines that are true and read them out loud.

Keep proof you were here.

Keys in the bowl.

Light by the sink.

Blinds open so morning can find you.

You learn the names of traps.

Hungry.

Angry.

Lonely.

Tired.

Feed the right one.

Call the right person.

Rest without apology.

Let quiet be medicine.

You stop asking small hands to hold a big heart.

You find wider hands.

A neighbor who waters plants at dawn.

A friend who says I am outside.

A room where late is not a sin.

You keep a chair open for the one who thinks they do not belong.

Sometimes that one is you.

You make amends where the bridge still stands.

You repair with action, not speeches.

Where the bridge is ash, you write a letter and let it rest.

You stop building museums to your worst day.

You build mornings instead.

You take another street that avoids the aisle that lies.

You turn down the song that turns your hands into strangers.

You put old numbers on a do not call list.

You choose stores with bright aisles and quick exits.

You choose hours that do not hunt you.

When the pew calls, you choose a bench outside.

You let the sun talk without words.

You count birds instead of sins.

You let your back touch the wood and remember you are carried.

When the gold cup glows, you read the fine print out loud.

Sleep first.

Friends next.

Health last.

You say no like a full sentence.

You pour water.

You sip slow.

You wait ten minutes and call a name you trust.

You keep a ledger of proofs.

Today I returned the cart.

Today I laughed from the middle, not the mask.

Today I was on time for my own life.

Today I told the truth before it hurt more.

Today I put the phone down at nine and slept.

You accept that some help is a fence.

You look for tables.

You accept that some blessings come with strings.

You keep your hands free.

You accept that you are not too much.

You are the size you had to be to survive.

Now you can learn another size.

You forgive the part of you that drank the gold.

You forgive the mouth that liked the silence.

You forgive the mind that called a cage a chapel.

You forgive, then you choose better furniture.

You speak softly to the heart that would not shrink.

You say thank you for staying loud.

You say I will build a place you fit.

You mean it.

If noon breaks you, try again at one.

If the pew feels safer than the circle, walk to the door and breathe.

If the gold flashes, read your list and call.

If no one answers, sit where you are and count to thirty.

Then call again.

Some people will keep the club small.

Let them.

You will keep the door open.

You will keep the light near the sink.

You will keep a spare key under the mat for the one who finally knocks.

Sometimes that is still you.

What can you do.

You live a life that fits.

You keep ties that hold without choking.

You let your heart take up its rightful space.

You drink from cups that do not charge your life at the end.

Sleep, and try.

Wake, and try.

Break, and try again when the hands are free.

This is the answer that does not glitter.

This is the prize that does not brag.

This is the hold that heals because it does not close.

NIGHT KNIGHT

I LIVED THROUGH THOUSANDS of nights.

I thought a guard stood watch.

I called him brave.

He came in a bottle and sat by the bed.

He kept the noise down for an hour.

He sent the bill in the morning.

I learned his rules.

Do not feel.

Do not ask.

Do not eat first.

Do not sleep on time.

I followed them until I forgot my own.

I took flight when feeling arrived.

Out of sight.

Out of reach.

I left messages on read.

I left rooms early.

I left myself for later and later never came.

The bite was real.

Jaw tight.

Stomach hot.

Hands that shook like I owed them money.

I called it stress.

It was the price.

All my might went to pretending.

I said I was fine.

I said I could stop.

I said this is the last time.

I said it again tomorrow.

My hands felt small.

They dropped promises I could not carry.

They fumbled keys.

They searched for phones I had put in my pocket.

They wanted to hold something that did not hurt.

Morning showed me its teeth.

Bright and honest.

It did not blink.

It asked who I planned to be today.

I did not have an answer, so I started small.

Water first.

Food next.

Four in.

Hold four.

Four out.

Repeat until the room calms down.

I wrote three lines that were true.

I read them out loud to hear my voice.

I cleaned the sink for the person I am in the morning.

I put the keys in the bowl.

I opened the blinds so light could find me.

I learned the names of traps.

Hungry.

Angry.

Lonely.

Tired.

I fed each without a speech.

I sat in a circle where chairs face each other.

First names.

Plain words.

Coffee that burns a little.

Sugar passed like trust.

No one fixed me.

They stayed.

I stayed too.

I called the ones who answered before.

I said the quiet part first.

I said I need help at noon, not at midnight.

They said come by.

They said I will meet you at the door.

I went.

I took another street.

I skipped the aisle that lies.

I turned down songs that turn my hands into strangers.

I put old numbers on a do not call list.

I chose stores with bright aisles and fast exits.

I made amends where the bridge still stands.

I used hands, not speeches.

Where the bridge is ash, I wrote a letter and let it rest.

I stopped building museums to my worst day.

I built mornings instead.

I kept a photo from before.

I looked at it with both eyes.

He is not a warning.

He is a measure of distance.

He proves the road is real.

Nights still arrive.

I do not pray to them.

I set the table.

Water by the lamp.

Phone facedown.

Room cool.

Breath like a metronome the body can trust.

When panic pops like bad fireworks, I plan for weather.

Walk to the corner.

Text the one who texts back.

Eat real food.

Call again if nobody answers.

Sit and count to thirty before I decide anything.

I kept a ledger of proofs.

Today I returned the cart.

SALT LINES

Today I was on time for my own life.
Today I told the truth before it hurt more.
Today I laughed and it sounded like me.
Thousands of lights showed me the door.
Streetlamps on late walks.
Phone screens with a name I can call.
Kitchen bulbs at 6 a.m. over clean counters.
A porch light left on for the latecomer.
Candles on a cake I did not think I would see.
Those lights pull us close.
They bring us tight.
They make rooms where no one has to hide.
They make a place for hearts that do not shrink.
If noon breaks me, I try again at one.
If the old guard calls, I read the bill out loud.
Everything.
I hang up.
I keep simple rules now.
Drink water first.
Say no like a sentence.
Say yes with both feet.
Keep a chair open.
Sometimes the latecomer is me.
I am not protected by a knight anymore.
I am kept by small work I can repeat.
Keys in the bowl.
Light by the sink.
Shoes by the door that still fit.

Thousands of nights taught me this.

I do not need a savior that bites.

I need a plan I can carry.

I need people who stay when I speak plainly.

I need light I can switch on with my own hand.

"

LYCAON

WE STOOD AND LOOKED down.

We said the name.

We let the room go quiet enough to hear it land.

The body did not argue.

Acceptance was in the air,

not as mercy, as gravity.

We learned the math of absence.

One gone.

Many gathered.

Tears came like weather.

Enough to drown if we forgot to breathe.

So we breathed.

Four in.

Hold four.

Four out.

Repeat until the hands stopped shaking.

Who knew the toll.

Not flowers.

Not speeches.

The price was carrying daylight without their laugh in it.

The price was walking out of the room and leaving them behind,

then walking back in and leaving them behind again.

Hearts went bare.

No armor.

No trick.

We let air touch the wound.

It stung.

It also kept the wound from rotting into stories that never end.

There were tasks that felt like betrayal and kindness at once.

Sign here.

Pick a time.

Choose a song.

Fold the programs down the middle.

Lay a tie flat.

Brush a collar smooth.

Cry over a button that would not close.

Give up.

Start again.

We found a new family in the hallways.

Quiet women with tissue and practical shoes.

Men who lifted chairs like they were lifting us.

Neighbors who knew where the coffee filters were kept.

A cousin who knew how to pronounce the hard names.

Someone who remembered extra pens.

SALT LINES

We counted the ways people say I love you without saying it.

Food arrived in dishes we had never seen.

Phones buzzed with gate codes and parking tips.

Someone took the dog for a long walk.

Someone watered plants we had forgotten we owned.

Someone moved the car before the tow truck had ideas.

At the graveside, the world shrunk to sound.

A shovel.

Soil.

A bird that refused to stop singing.

We hated the bird for three seconds.

Then we loved it for trying.

One buried whole.

The rest learned to live with holes.

We did not fill them with noise.

We lined them with names

and sat near.

Life is unfair.

The sentence is a fact, not a verdict.

We did not argue with it.

We argued with ourselves about where to sit,

what to eat,

who to call first,

and then we called.

We practiced the ordinary as if it were sacred.

Keys in the bowl.

Light by the sink.

Shoes near the door that still fit.

Water before coffee.

Food with color.

Three lines on paper that are true enough to read aloud.

We kept a ledger of proof that the day happened.

We returned the cart.

We turned off the stove.

We opened the blinds.

We answered a message with the words I am here.

We believed it for thirty seconds.

We believed it again for thirty more.

The pew was full.

We sat at the edge for quick exits.

We learned to nod when the old words did not fit.

We learned to close our eyes when they did.

We did not pretend to be strong.

We pretended to be sitting,

and that was enough.

We spoke in first names.

We avoided stories that made heroes out of pain.

We avoided stories that made villains out of tears.

We told the simple version.

He lived.

We loved.

He died.

We still love.

This is the part where we keep going.

At the table afterward, grief moved like a person.

It took the good chair.

It ate without asking.

We made room for it anyway.

We poured coffee for it too.

We kept sugar on the table.

We passed the cream.

A new family took shape in the small work.

Fold a blanket.

Find an outlet.

Call the florist before noon.

Tell the aunt the address again.

Make space for the cousin who arrives late on purpose.

She will stand in the doorway and need to be told twice that she is not too late.

She is not too late.

In the nights that followed, we heard the old offer.

Something warm that promised to soften the edges.

A cup that glowed like a solution.

We read the receipt out loud.

Sleep first.

Friends next.

Health last.

We put the cup down.

We poured water.

We waited ten minutes and called a name we trust.

We learned the names of our hungers.

Hungry.

Angry.

Lonely.

Tired.

We fed each the right thing.

Food.

Quiet.

Company.

Sleep.

We did not feed grief with what would make it louder.

We sat in chairs that face each other.

Not an altar.

A circle.

A coffee pot that burns a little.

A spoon that has seen things.

We said our names like we meant to keep them.

We told the truth in short sentences.

Nobody fixed anybody.

We stayed.

We made amends with the living because death reminds you to hurry.

We apologized where the bridge still stood.

We used hands, not speeches.

Where the bridge was ash, we wrote letters and let them rest.

We stopped building museums to mistakes.

We built mornings instead.

We carried photos like pocket maps.

We looked with both eyes.

We did not turn them into warnings.

We turned them into distance markers.

Look how far we have walked since this smile.

We let the unfairness breathe without giving it the last word.

We let the last word be practice.

Breath in four.

Hold.

Out four.

Again.

We let the last word be presence.

I am here.

Say it out loud.

Hear it come back.

There were days the house felt too big.

We closed the extra door.

We used only one room and did not feel like we were losing.

We slept in the bed that was ours.

We left a cup by the lamp.

We trusted our bodies enough to let them rest.

We kept a chair open at the table.

We did not pretend it was not empty.

We left it empty on purpose.

We talked to the space when we needed to.

We laughed at something they would have mocked.

We cried when we had to.

We did not apologize to the air.

We learned the emergency plan for the heart.

Call first.

Walk to the corner.

Drink water.

Eat something.

Count to thirty before deciding anything permanent.

If nobody answers, call again.

If the call fails, sit where you are until the room gets bigger.

When noon broke us, we tried again at one.

When morning felt like a dare, we got up anyway.

When night asked for stories we could not tell yet,

we said later and meant it.

We did not become saints.

We became consistent.

We kept ties that hold without choking.

We let help be as ordinary as taking out the trash.

We let love be as plain as showing up on time.

We looked down and said goodbye,

which is a hard word for stay with me in another way.

We looked up and said hello to the day that still expects something
of us.

We met it with small good things.

Keys in the bowl.

Light by the sink.

Shoes by the door that still fit.

A new family found us because we were findable.

One buried whole.

The rest learned to shoulder holes without pretending they are not
there.

Life is unfair.

We are not undone.

Sleep, and we will try.

Wake, and we will try.

Break, and we will try again when the hands are free.

Say the name when you need to.

Say your own when you forget.

Breathe.

Eat.

Call.

Walk.

Write three lines of something true.

This is how we pay the toll without losing the road.

This is how we keep what cannot be taken.

This is how we carry the dead without setting ourselves down.

THE FALL

Victory among us.

Not banners.

Not drums.

A nod across a small room.

A clap that lands like breath returning.

Legends cried out once.

Tonight they smile and pour coffee.

They point to chairs.

They point to tomorrow.

Home fills with lust after the bout.

Not bodies.

The old cup glowing like a solution.

The song that used to own my feet.

A bottle practicing my name in the dark.

I read the price out loud.

Sleep first.

SALT LINES

Friends next.

Health last.

I put the cup down.

I pour water.

I wait ten minutes and call.

Redemption is not a parade.

It is the cool air on the porch at dusk.

It is a lung that remembers its size.

Four in.

Hold four.

Four out.

Repeat until the hands stop shaking.

I listen to crickets count for me.

I let quiet do the first round of work.

A family seized, the line says.

I know the feeling.

Grief grabs.

Debt calls.

We pay what we can with money, with time, with new behavior.

We carry casseroles in borrowed dishes.

We fold chairs.

We water plants we forgot we owned.

We make amends where the bridge still stands.

Hands, not speeches.

Where the bridge is ash, we write a letter and let it rest.

Victory is small and repeats.

Keys in the bowl.

Light by the sink.

Shoes by the door that still fit.

Water before coffee.

Food with color.

Three lines on paper I can read out loud.

I return the cart.

I answer the text.

I do not hide the bill.

The mighty warriors are plain people.

They carry grocery bags and spare batteries.

They keep a spare key under the mat for the latecomer.

Sometimes the latecomer is me.

They say sit.

They say we started without you and saved a seat.

I sit.

I stay.

The cabin we built from lies will fall.

Let it.

The roof goes first.

Grand proclamations.

Personal myths.

The smoke that says I am fine.

We stand outside with a garden hose of truth.

We keep distance.

We save what matters.

Photos.

Names.

A dog who wants out now.

Flames burn from the top.

They do not reach the footings we poured this year.

Food on a schedule.

Sleep like a duty.

Routes that skip the aisle that lies.

Songs that keep my hands mine.

Numbers on a do not call list.

A plan for loud hours.

Walk at three.

Text at seven.

Bed before ten.

Home tries to be loud again.

I answer with ordinary.

Dishes rinsed.

Counters wiped.

Tomorrow's cup waiting by the sink.

The body trusts me when I keep these promises.

The mind follows when the body leads.

I keep the hunger list near.

Hungry.

Angry.

Lonely.

Tired.

Feed the right one.

Call the right person.

Sit with company that does not sell anything.

Rest without apology.

I keep a photo from before.

I look with both eyes.

He is not a warning.

He is a distance marker.

He proves the road is real because I have walked it.

We pay our debts and stop worshiping the ledger.

We thank the clerk who says see you tomorrow.

We make tomorrow a promise we intend to keep.

We keep it with small proof.

On time.

Polite.

Present.

The legends still cry out, but softer.

Live.

Drink water first.

Say no like a sentence.

Say yes with both feet.

Keep a chair open.

If noon breaks me, I try again at one.

If the song returns, I turn up the lights I can move.

Phone a friend.

Open the blinds.

Walk to the corner.

Back again.

Write three lines that are true enough to steady me.

Mighty warriors atop sounds grand.

I think of us on the steps after the meeting.

Paper cups.

Jokes about weak coffee.

A plan for Tuesday that fits in a pocket.

Breathe.

Call.

Eat.

Sleep.

The mighty cabin falls.

Good.

We needed space for something that does not burn.

A table that seats whoever shows up.

A porch light we leave on.

A door that opens from both sides.

The flames eat the roof and move on.

We do not.

We stay.

We sweep.

We stack lumber that will not lie to us.

We level the frame with truth and time.

Thousands of lights answer the night.

Streetlamps on late walks.

Kitchen bulbs at six over clean counters.

Phone screens with names we can call.

Candles on cakes we did not think we would see.

They bring us tight.

They make a circle we can stand inside.

Victory calls.

Not loud.

Steady.

It sounds like a kettle settling.

Like keys on wood.

Like a dog turning once before sleep.

It sounds like our own names, said by people who plan to stay.

Sleep, and we try again.

Wake, and we try again.

Break, and we try again when the hands are free.

This is the bout we win by staying.

This is the legend we earn by living.

This is the home we fill with what lasts.

ABOUT THE AUTHOR

T.B. WITTKOFSKY IS A storyteller, educator, and community builder who uses his personal experiences to help others rise with their stories. With a background in marketing, communications, and mental health advocacy, his work blends strategy with heart. T.B. has taught courses on branding, social media, and entrepreneurship, guiding students and creatives through the evolving digital landscape.

After overcoming challenges like addiction, job loss, and financial instability, T.B. embraced a life on the road in an RV with his wife and three dogs, finding clarity, healing, and inspiration in the journey. He now leads Adventure with Coffee, a blog and podcast that celebrates connection through culture, travel, and, of course, coffee.

As the former president of the North Brunswick Chamber of Commerce and founder of Tea With Coffee Media, T.B. has helped countless entrepreneurs and small businesses find their voice. His advocacy work, including panels on mental health and representation in fiction, underscores his mission to create safe, inclusive spaces for honest storytelling.

Whether mentoring writers, consulting on marketing campaigns, or writing stories that reflect lived truths, T.B. shows up with compassion, curiosity, and an unwavering belief in the power of the narrative.

Other Works

(Not) Alone
A Mental Health Novella

Coffee, Alcohol, and Heartbreak:
A Poetry Collection

The Principal's Principles
Literary Fiction Based on a True Story

The Sunflower Kisses Series
A Man's POV Romance

Book 1: The Seeds of Love

Enamored Echoes (with Kelsey Anne Lovelady)
Romantic Fantasy Series

Book 1: Potent